Sugar Inspirations

Creative Cutter Designs

ANNE WHITE

MEREHURST

Dedication

To the memory of my mother, who always believed in me.

First published 1998 by Merehurst Limited
Ferry House, 51–57 Lacy Road, Putney,
London SW15 1PR

Copyright © Merehurst Limited 1998
ISBN 1-85391-707-9

A catalogue record for this book is available from the
British Library.

Editor: Helen Southall
Design: Anita Ruddell
Photography by Clive Streeter

Colour separation by Bright Arts, Hong Kong
Printed in Hong Kong by Wing King Tong

Contents

Introduction

Simple and quick, cutters can be used to create cake designs that are as attractive as the finest piping.

The continuing growth of interest in cake decoration has encouraged manufacturers of cake decorating equipment to produce more and more new cutters, so that there is now a bewildering selection of cutters on the market. Gone are the days when we carefully dissected flowers and made templates of each petal, all carefully labelled with instructions on how to reassemble the flower in sugar. The advent of lace cutters also means that the hours and hours spent piping lace pieces on to waxed paper, and breaking every other one during the assembly on the cake, are a thing of the past. While we cannot possibly hope to emulate the delicate work we all admire at exhibitions and other displays, we can still produce fine, attractive lace using cutters. See, for example, the peacock cake on page 27.

It is certainly less time-consuming to purchase a ready-made cutter, but this often leaves us with boxes full of cutters that we may only use once or twice. By doing a bit of 'lateral thinking' and using our imaginations, however, we can bring these cutters back into use for other designs and techniques. It is great fun to take a cutter and a piece of flower or modelling paste and to 'play' with them to see how many different shapes and ideas one can produce!

This book is intended to stimulate new ideas, and to help you get the best use from your cutters in producing original and innovative designs. We are all individuals and have our own interests and enthusiasms. If these are at the heart of the work we produce it will be truly creative and carry a personal value. Don't be afraid to experiment; you can always eat your mistakes!

Techniques

Rolling out paste

As a general rule, roll the paste out very thinly as some cutters are very detailed and will block if the paste is too thick. Keep the paste covered as much as possible while working as it dries out quickly.

Using new cutters

Read the manufacturer's instructions as many give specific paste recipes and advise the use of a certain type of vegetable fat (shortening). Success can be ensured by following the guidelines provided.

Embossing

Embossing techniques are used to mark the outline of a design on to soft paste, without actually cutting it out. Practise on a spare piece of sugarpaste (rolled fondant) first. With a little practice you will be able to apply this technique directly on to the cake without a template. When embossing, lift the cutter from the paste by the handle to prevent fingermarks.

Experimenting with cutter shapes

When planning a new design, it is helpful to make a template of the top and sides of the cake. Draw around the cutters you wish to use and cut out in paper or thin card. You can then move the pieces around on the templates to see how your ideas work.

Using colour

Almond paste (marzipan), royal icing, sugarpaste (rolled fondant), flower paste and mexican paste can all be coloured, as required, using paste food colours. Cut-out pieces of paste can be coloured by dusting with edible dusting powders (petal dusts/blossom tints). They can also be painted with paste or powder colours diluted with alcohol, or they can be air-brushed with liquid colours, either on or off the cake. Marbled effects can be achieved by mixing two or more coloured pastes together.

Tools and Equipment

Ruler
Pencil
Scriber
Tweezers
Rolling pin
Dresden tool
Tracing paper
Non-stick board
Selection of cutters
Cranked palette knife
Straight palette knife
Scalpel or craft knife
Thin card for templates
Small pair of sharp scissors
Tilting turntable for working on sides of cakes
Selection of formers for producing curved pieces

Some of the designs in this book make use of particular makes and types of cutter, all of which are available from the suppliers listed on page 48. For identification purposes, the numbers of the cutters used and the initials of the relevant manufacturer are given with each design. The cake designs are, however, intended to be flexible and can be adapted according to your own ideas and the cutters you already have.

Basic Recipes

Mexican Paste (1)

This is a very elastic paste, which sets and dries hard. It is ideal for pieces that need to be strong or that will be handled more than usual. This is the paste to use whenever mexican paste is required in the designs in this book, unless otherwise stated.

250g (8oz/1½ cups) icing (confectioner's) sugar, sifted
3 teaspoons gum tragacanth or gum tragacanth substitute (CMC)
2 teaspoons liquid glucose
6–7 teaspoons cold water

1 Sift the icing sugar and gum tragacanth together on to a work surface and form a well in the centre. Add the liquid glucose and 6 teaspoons water. Mix all the ingredients together. Add the remaining teaspoon of water if the paste appears dry or is crumbly. Knead well until the ingredients are well blended and the paste is smooth.

2 Divide the paste into four portions. Place in plastic bags and seal in an air-tight container. Store in a cool place for up to 6 weeks.

Mexican Paste (2)

This will give a softer, more pliable paste that does not set quite so hard as Mexican Paste (1). It is suitable for appliqué and smocking work. Sugarpaste (rolled fondant) is available from supermarkets and cake decorating suppliers.

Equal quantities of Mexican Paste (1), page 5, and sugarpaste (rolled fondant)

 1 Mix the two pastes thoroughly together.

2 Divide the paste into four portions. Place in plastic bags and seal in an airtight container. Store in a cool place for up to 3 months.

Marzipan Modelling Paste

Ready-made shop-bought almond paste (marzipan) is a smooth modelling paste that gives good results. White almond paste provides a more neutral colour base if you wish to add colouring before use. The addition of gum tragacanth helps the paste to harden and remain hard once dry.

250g (8oz) almond paste (marzipan)
1 teaspoon gum tragacanth or gum tragacanth substitute (CMC)

1 Knead the paste well. Add the gum tragacanth and knead well again to ensure all the powder is well worked into the paste.

2 Place the paste in a plastic bag and store for at least 1 hour before using.

3 Add paste colour as required and knead well. Allow to stand for 1 hour for the colour to develop before using.

4 Roll out the paste using a little sifted icing (confectioner's) sugar to prevent sticking. Stick pieces together with a little royal icing.

Sugar Glue

This is useful for sticking mexican paste or sugarpaste (rolled fondant) pieces together.

155ml (5fl oz/⅔ cup) cold water
30g (1oz) sugarpaste (rolled fondant), broken into pieces
3 teaspoons clear alcohol (vodka or white rum)

1 Place the water and sugarpaste pieces in a small heatproof bowl and microwave on high for approximately 30 seconds. Alternatively, place the bowl over a saucepan of boiling water and stir until softened.

2 Sieve the mixture into another bowl, add the alcohol and stir well. Transfer to a clean jug and store in a cool place or the refrigerator.

Creative Cutting

There are very few subjects which cannot be reproduced using cutters in one way or another. You are limited only by your imagination. The following are just a few ideas.

1 Round cutters in different sizes give endless variations of faces and cartoon characters. These can be cut out of finely rolled paste and used as appliqué or cut out of thicker paste and used to create a bas-relief effect.

2 Cut out a shape with your chosen cutter. Move the same cutter, or another one, across the piece of paste to cut out another, different shape.

3 Oval, round and teardrop-shaped cutters of different sizes give numerous curved and crescent shapes, useful for sickle moons, etc. They can also be used to make bridges for extension work.

4 Turning a cutter upside-down can give a different shape altogether.

5 With more intricate cutters, cut out the design in paste and then remove areas of the cut-out piece with a knife to reduce the size of it or to separate just one part of the design. The removed pieces can be used to make another pattern or to complement the main design, perhaps on the sides of the cake or board.

6 Cutting a second shape out of the centre of the first shape can create a lace effect.

7 Lace cutters can be used to make edging frills, etc., but can also be used for creating other forms of decorations, finishing edges or plaques, Easter eggs, crenellations on churches, gable ends on houses, fretwork, weather-boarding, etc.

8 Plastic cutters are useful for embossing designs directly on to fresh sugarpasted surfaces. Sketch out a rough template of the area to be decorated, to give you a guide for the positioning of the cutters.

9 Rubbing the cutter in powder colouring can give a coloured edging to your embossed pattern. (Practise first.) Two or more colours can be used.

10 Cut out the same shape several times and superimpose the pieces to create a découpage effect, or to fix together to make a three-dimensional standing figure.

11 Pointed multi-petal cutters can be used to make collars and hats.

12 Blunt-edged multi-petal cutters, such as daisies, can be used to cut out pieces that will interlock and form cogs for engines, clocks, etc.

13 Carnation/blossom cutters can be used for hair. Carnation cutters with the centres removed will make miniature Garrett frills, useful for edging skirts, etc.

14 Clouds can be created using large blossom and round cutters.

15 Small/miniature cutters can be used to cut out pieces from larger cut-outs to create a fretwork or trellis effect. Pillars and spacers can be made in this way.

16 Geometric cutters can be used to create mosaic and patchwork.

17 Leaf shapes in different colours can be overlaid to produce interesting scenery.

18 Leaf shapes can be textured and curved to form feathers and birds' wings.

19 Individual cut-out and dried pieces can be overlapped on to the top edge of a cake to form a collar. This can be piped with royal icing.

20 Combine several techniques using one cutter. Emboss, then cut out flat shapes, then cut out and curve the same shapes. All arranged together, these can give a new dimension to your design.

21 Multi-petal cutter shapes set in convex moulds can form containers for all sorts of items, such as small marzipan (almond paste) fruits, sweets, sugar eggs, even babies (in sugar of course!).

22 Small petal shapes make attractive tiles or slates to use on roofs, etc.

Embossed Ivy Leaf Cake

This pretty cake uses plastic cutters for embossing and outlining, try to draw the stem lines on to the cake freehand.

Materials

20cm (8 inch) round cake
Apricot glaze
750g (1½ lb) almond paste
(marzipan)
1kg (2lb) ivory sugarpaste
(rolled fondant)
250g (8oz/1 cup) ivory royal
icing
Selection of powder food colours
(petal dusts/blossom tints)
Clear alcohol (vodka or white
rum)

Equipment

25cm (10 inch) round cake
board
Crimper
Nos. 0, 1 and 2 piping tubes
(tips)
Piping bags
Scriber or dresden tool
Nos. 0 and 1 paintbrushes

Cutters

Medium and small ivy leaf
cutters (OP, IV3, IV4)
Mini calyx cutter (OP, R15)
Medium 6-petal flower cutter
(OP, N6)
Small rose leaf cutter (OP, R7)

Preparation

1 Coat the cake board with ivory sugarpaste and crimp the edges. Brush the cake with apricot glaze and cover with almond paste. Coat with ivory sugarpaste and set on the board. With a no. 2 piping tube and ivory royal icing, pipe a snail's trail to seal the cake to the board.

2 With a scriber or the pointed end of a dresden tool, lightly 'draw' some stem lines in the soft sugarpaste on the sides and top of the cake. Use long sweeping strokes to create natural curves. You could also scribe some stems on the board around the base of the cake, if you wish.

> **5** Small joining stems and veins can now be marked in with the scriber or pointed end of the dresden tool.

Painting

> **6** Using a fine paintbrush, mix the powder colour of your choice with a little clear alcohol to form a paste. This will give a clear colour; if you wish to use an opaque colour, add a small amount of white powder colour to the mixture.

> **7** Using firm brush strokes, paint in the design, remembering to follow the natural lines of veins in leaves, etc.

> **8** To complete the cake, pipe in a few fine lines and dots with a no. 0 or 1 piping tube and ivory royal icing.

Embossing

> **3** Put a selection of powder colours on to a plate or other flat surface. Holding each cutter in turn by its handle, gently rub it into the powder colour of your choice. You can use one or more colours at a time to create a shaded effect.

> **4** Tap off any excess colour and carefully press the colour-loaded cutter into the soft paste on the cake. This will give the embossed shapes a delicately coloured edging. If you prefer a plain finish, use the cutters without dipping them into colour first. Continue in this way with all the cutters until you have completed your design.

Springtime

Delicate bluebells trim the side of this cake with its unusual floral design. Other flower cutters could be used to create a similar cake, perhaps for Christmas or autumn.

Materials

20cm (8 inch) oval cake
Apricot glaze
750g (1½ lb) almond paste (marzipan)
750g (1½ lb) ivory sugarpaste (rolled fondant)
250g (8oz) pale green sugar-paste (rolled fondant)
250g (8oz) mexican paste
250g (8oz/1 cup) royal icing
Selection of paste and powder food colours, including green, yellow, pink and blue
Clear alcohol (vodka or white rum)

Equipment

30cm (12 inch) oval cake board
Tracing paper and pencil
Thin card for template
Craft knife or scalpel
Smoother
Nos. 1, 1.5 and 2 piping tubes (tips)
Piping bags
Paintbrushes

Cutters

Spring flowers cutter/embosser (PC)

Preparation

1 Brush the cake with apricot glaze and cover with almond paste. Allow to set for 24 hours. Coat the cake board with ivory sugarpaste and allow to set.

Side inset

2 Trace the side inset template on page 47 and transfer to thin card. Cut out.

3 Roll out green sugarpaste and coat the side of the cake only. Hold the card template against the cake side and cut the green sugarpaste around it with a sharp knife. Remove the paste from above the inset.

4 Coat the remainder of the cake with ivory sugar-paste and cut away surplus so that it fits neatly above the green sugarpaste. Smooth over the join between the two colours. Place the cake on the sugarpasted board. Using pale green royal icing and a no. 2 piping tube, pipe a snail's trail to seal the base of the cake to the board.

Floral design

5 Press the spring flowers cutter on to the side and

8 When the brush embroidery is dry, fix the loose flowers and petals to the embossed patterns with a little royal icing, gradually building up the designs.

9 Using powder colours mixed with clear alcohol, paint the flowers and allow to dry. Paint the bluebells in the same way and allow to dry.

top of the cake to emboss the pattern.

6 Roll out some mexican paste thinly and cut out the flower pattern several times. (The paste can be coloured or left white and painted afterwards.) Separate the flowers with a sharp knife. Curve and shape some of them and allow all the pieces to dry. You will need approximately 18 bluebell pieces for the edging.

10 With a little royal icing, fix the bluebells along the join in the sugarpaste on the side of the cake, and continue around the base. To finish the decoration, pipe dots in ivory royal icing with a no. 1 tube along the top of the side inset, and in groups around the flowers.

7 With ivory royal icing, a no.1.5 piping tube and a small paintbrush, brush-embroider the outer parts of the embossed designs on the cake: pipe the outline of the flowers and, with a slightly dampened brush, draw the icing across the surface to achieve a textured effect. The outside piped edge should remain unbroken and the surface covered in a thin layer of coloured sugar. Leave to dry.

Smocking Cake

These delightful little girls are easily made using cutters, the flowers are cut from multi-flower cutters, and a smocking cutter is used for the sides.

Materials

20cm (8 inch) octagonal cake
Apricot glaze
750g (1½lb) almond paste (marzipan)
1kg (2lb) white sugarpaste (rolled fondant)
750g (1½lb) Mexican Paste (2), see page 6
250g (8oz/1 cup) royal icing
Selection of paste and powder food colours, including pink, black and flesh
Sugar glue
Clear alcohol (vodka or white rum)

Equipment

25cm (10 inch) octagonal cake board
Crimper
Tracing paper and pencil
Scriber
Dresden tool
Cocktail stick (toothpick)
Paintbrushes
Craft knife or scalpel
Nos. 0 and 1 piping tubes (tips)
Piping bags
Ruler

Cutters

Small bell cutter (CA, 81066)
Large petal cutter
Small round cutter

Ribbon cutter (FCC)
Multi-flower cutters (PC)
Smocking embosser/cutter (PC)

Preparation

1 Coat the cake board with white sugarpaste and crimp the edges. Brush the cake with apricot glaze and coat with almond paste. Cover with white sugarpaste and allow to set for 24 hours. Place the cake in the centre of the board.

2 Colour 375g (12oz) of the mexican paste pale pink and place in a plastic bag. Colour the remainder of the paste in different colours, including white and flesh, for the top decoration.

Top decoration

3 Trace the template on page 46, and transfer the outline to the top of the cake with a scriber. (The decoration could be worked on a plaque and placed on the cake afterwards, if you prefer.)

4 Make the arms and hands from small sausages of flesh-coloured paste. Keep all the pieces covered until ready to position on the cake.

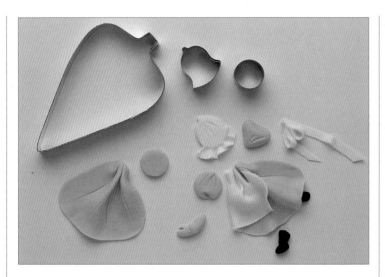

8 Place the apron over the skirt, and adjust the gathers with the dresden tool. Remove any excess paste you may have at the top point of the figure.

9 Next, fix the sleeve and right arm into position, then attach the bonnet to the figure, placing a small piece of paste under the crown to make it rounded. Make tiny shoes in black paste and slip them under the skirt hem so that they just show.

10 Complete the figure on the right in the same way, and finally complete the central figure.

11 When all the figures are finished, roll out some white mexican paste very thinly and cut some strips with the ribbon cutter. Fold over the top ends of the strips and attach one across the other to make bows. Attach to the backs of the skirts with the ends trailing.

12 Thinly roll out some more mexican paste and cut out the flower patterns several

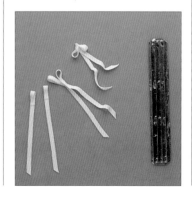

5 Cut out white bonnets with the small bell cutter, and indent gathers at the crowns and bases with a dresden tool, slightly stretching the paste at the bottom edge to form a frill. Keep covered.

6 Using the large petal cutter, cut out skirts and aprons, and again indent gathers and pleats where necessary. Use the small round cutter to make sleeves from slightly thicker paste. Indent gathers. Keep all pieces covered.

7 Working from the 'back' of the picture, i.e. the furthest point away from you, build up the figures in stages, sticking the pieces of paste to the surface of the cake with sugar glue: start with the figure on the left of the picture, and fix the left hand and arm first, then attach the skirt, lifting the bottom hem slightly to create some movement. You could make a small frill (by rolling a strip of paste with a cocktail stick) and slip it underneath the hem to represent a petticoat.

times. With a sharp knife, remove the pieces you require, colour them, and attach them to the cake with a little sugar glue. Finish the top decoration by piping curly lines and dots of pale yellow royal icing, using a no. 1 piping tube.

Smocking

13 Measure the width and depth of the side panels on the cake. Roll out some pink mexican paste and emboss the smocking pattern on to the paste with the smocking cutter.

14 Covering one panel at a time, cut out a piece of smocking of the required size with a ruler and sharp knife. Brush the side of the cake with sugar glue and fix the smocked panel into position, taking care not to stretch the paste. Continue in this way until all sides are complete with panels.

15 Thinly roll out some more pink paste and cut several strips the same lengths as the tops of the panels and approximately 1cm (½ inch) wide. Frill one edge of each strip with a cocktail stick or the handle of a paintbrush.

16 Fix the frilled strips to the top and bottom edges of the smocked panels with sugar glue.

17 With a no. 0 piping tube and white royal icing, pipe small lines and dots on to the smocked panels, following the

pattern, to represent stitching. Make some paste bows as before

(see Step 11) and fix between the panels with royal icing.

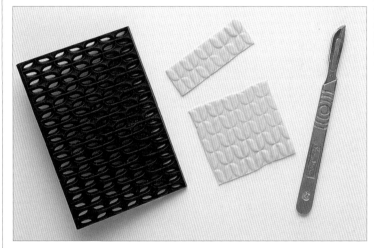

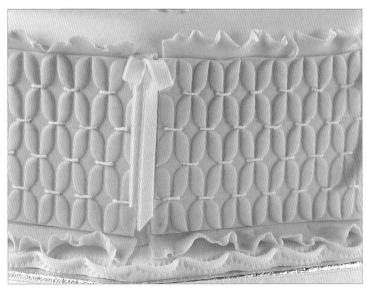

17

Sunflower Faces

Bright sunflowers with smiling faces will bring a touch of summer to your celebration. Any large multi-petal cutter could be used.

Materials

25cm (10 inch) round cake
Apricot glaze
1kg (2lb) almond paste (marzi-pan)
1kg (2lb) deep cream coloured sugarpaste (rolled fondant)
90g (3oz) white sugarpaste
250g (8oz/1 cup) deep cream coloured royal icing
500g (1lb) mexican paste
Selection of paste and powder food colours, including flesh, cream and shades of yellow/gold
Sugar glue
Clear alcohol (vodka or white rum)

Equipment

30cm (12 inch) round cake board
Crimpers
No. 2 piping tube (tip)
Piping bags
Ball tool
Dresden tool
Pieces of foam
Paintbrushes
Scalpel or sharp knife

Cutters

Large sunflower cutter (FCC, 678)
Small oval cutter (FCC, 493)

Preparation

1 Coat the cake board with cream sugarpaste and crimp the edge if desired.

2 Cut approximately 7.5cm (3 inches) from one side of the cake so that it can stand on its side. Brush the top and curved side of the cake with apricot glaze and cover with almond paste. Allow to set for 24 hours.

3 Turn the cake over carefully on to greaseproof paper and cover the other flat side with almond paste as before. Allow to set for 24 hours.

4 Coat both flat sides and the curved edge of the cake with cream sugarpaste. Set the cake on its flat side on the board and neaten the sugarpaste joins with crimpers. Using cream royal icing and a no. 2 piping tube, pipe a snail's trail around the base of the cake.

Sunflowers

5 Mix 90g (3oz) mexican paste with the white sugarpaste. Colour this paste a pale flesh colour and store in a plastic bag. Colour the remainder of the mexican paste in different shades of yellow.

6 Roll out the yellow pastes and cut out approximately 12 sunflowers. Soften the edges with a ball tool and mark veins with a dresden tool. Allow the flowers to set slightly, but they should still be pliable when you attach them to the cake.

7 Attach the sunflowers to the cake with a little

cream royal icing.
You will need to lift and curve some of the petals so that they overlap and the flowers almost cover the surface. Allow some of them to stand up over the top edge and others to curve round on to the board. Some of the petals may need to be supported with pieces of foam while they are drying.

Faces

8 Roll out the flesh-coloured paste to approximately 2.5mm (⅛ inch) thick and cut out the basic face shapes with a small oval cutter. Using your fingertips, smooth the edges and contour the shapes. Small pieces of paste can be tucked underneath to form cheeks, if necessary.

9 Make the noses from tiny cones of paste, attach them to the faces with a little sugar glue and blend them on to the face with a fine paintbrush. Nostrils can be marked in with the fine point of the dresden tool. Eye sockets can be indented and 'eye balls' added using tiny pieces of white paste. Alternatively, the eyes can be painted in.

10 While the faces are still slightly soft, fix them to the sunflower centres with a little royal icing. Smooth into position and allow to dry. Paint in facial details with a paintbrush and pale brown food colour diluted with a little clear alcohol. By painting with a pale colour first you can erase any mistakes with a damp brush. When you are satisfied with the results, you can emphasize the features with a stronger colour.

11 Finish the faces off by adding hair, hats, collars, ties and bows. These can be piped with royal icing and brushed with a damp brush to give texture, or soft mexican paste could be used. Try to give each face a different character, perhaps modelled on members of the family! Leave the back of the cake plain or cover with more sunflowers.

Rose Petal Cake

This teardrop-shaped cake was inspired by the 1900s' fashion for stylized flower decoration. By using different-sized cutters in conjunction, endless permutations of shapes are possible.

Materials

25cm (10 inch) teardrop-shaped cake
Apricot glaze
1.25kg (2½lb) almond paste (marzipan)
1.25kg (2½lb) white sugarpaste (rolled fondant)
250g (8oz) mexican paste
250g (8oz/1 cup) royal icing
Lavender, green, blue and pink paste food colours
Sugar glue

Equipment

36cm (14 inch) oval cake board
Nos. 1, 1.5 and 2 piping tubes (tips)
Piping bags
Tracing paper and pencil
Scriber
Tilting turntable
Craft knife or scalpel

Cutters

Ribbon cutter (FCC, 245)
Stainless steel rose petal cutter set (PME, RP190)

Preparation

1 Brush the cake with apricot glaze and cover with almond paste. Coat with white sugarpaste and allow to dry for 24 hours. Coat the cake board with white sugarpaste and allow to set for 24 hours.

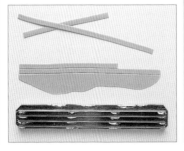

Board decoration

2 Divide the mexican paste into four portions and colour them lavender, pale green, pale blue and pale pink.

3 Roll out and cut strips of mexican paste with the ribbon cutter and fix them to the board with sugar glue, following the design illustrated on page 23 or a design of your own.

4 Place the cake on the board. Using a no. 2 piping tube and royal icing, pipe a snail's trail around the base of the cake.

Cake decoration

5 Prepare a paper template of the top of the cake and sketch or trace on to it your chosen design, showing the positions of the appliquéd flowers and leaves. Templates for the design illustrated are given on page 46. Place the paper template on the cake and mark guidelines with a scriber.

6 Place the cake on a tilting turntable and tilt it away from you. Roll out and cut more strips of blue mexican paste with the ribbon cutter and fix to the sides of the cake with a little sugar glue, turning the cake as necessary.

7 Roll out pale pink and lavender mexican paste and cut out petal shapes. Using the different-sized cutters, cut the petals into shaped pieces, as illustrated above. Fix to the cake with sugar glue. It may help to plan the shape of each flower before fixing it to the cake.

8 Cut out more petal shapes of green mexican paste and fix to the cake for leaves. Keep all the appliqué pieces as flat as possible with the edges clean and sharp. Press them gently into position without denting the paste.

9 Using deep lavender coloured royal icing and a no. 1.5 piping tube, pipe in the stems of the flowers and leaves. Using a no. 1 tube, overpipe the edges of the flowers and leaves.

Winter Frost

This all-white cake is finished with a final dusting of edible frosted colour to give it a real sparkle. Any large 'spikey' cutters could give a similar effect to the leaves.

Materials

15cm (6 inch) round cake
Apricot glaze
750g (1½lb) almond paste (marzipan)
750g (1½lb) white sugarpaste (rolled fondant)
500g (1lb) mexican paste
250g (8oz/1 cup) white royal icing
White edible frosted powder colour (petal dust/blossom tint)

Equipment

25cm (10 inch) round cake board
Tracing paper and pencil
Thin card for templates and formers
15cm (6 inch) round polystyrene dummy cake (for former)
Craft knife or scalpel
Large plastic scraper or heavy-duty card
Plastic side scraper
Nos. 1 and 2 piping tubes (tips)
Piping bags
Large soft paintbrush for dusting

Cutters

Large ivy leaf cutter (CC, L13)
Green heuchera leaf cutter (CC, L30)

Preparation

1 Brush the cake with apricot glaze and cover with almond paste. Allow to dry for 24 hours. Cover the cake and board with sugarpaste and allow to dry for 24 hours. Place the cake on the board.

Background scenery

2 Make a template for the background (see pages 46–47), trace on to thin card and cut out. Cut the dummy cake crossways in half and fix the two halves together, one on top of the other, lining up the straight, cut sides. Place, cut side down, on a flat surface.

3 Roll out some mexican paste and cut out the background scenery using the template. Cut a leaf shape out of the background with the large ivy leaf cutter. Using a large plastic scraper or heavy-duty card, carefully lift the piece and lay it over the former, pressing it in gently against the sides. Allow to dry for 48 hours.

Snowflake effects

4 Roll out more mexican paste thinly and cut out ivy and heuchera leaves. With a plastic side scraper, gently mark fold lines on the leaves, and fold and pleat them zig-zag fashion

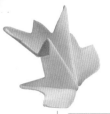

(as shown in the above photographs) to create snowflake shapes. Be careful not to press too hard and split the paste. Make some flat leaves as well. Allow to dry for 24 hours. It may help to place the leaves in a folded card to set, depending on how tight you want the folds to be. Allow some to dry in loose, others in tight, folds to create large and small snowflakes.

Assembly

5 Fix the scenery to the back of the cake with a little royal icing. Fix the pleated leaves to the cake and scenery in the same way. You may find that the leaves will interlock at some points. Allow to dry. Using a no. 2 piping tube and white royal icing, pipe a small snail's trail to neaten the join between the cake and the board. Allow to dry.

6 Using a no. 1 piping tube and white royal icing, add small piped dots to the cake's surface, and allow to dry. Dust with frosted dusting powder for a final gleam!

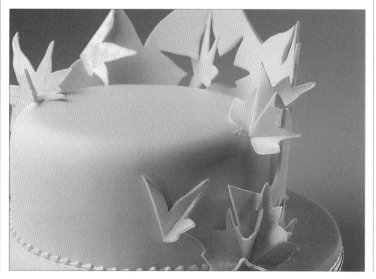

Twin Peacocks

The intertwining tails of these beautiful white peacocks are created using a classic lace leaf pattern. Long leaf cutters could be used to create a similar effect.

Materials

20cm (8 inch) round cake
Apricot glaze
750g (1½lb) almond paste (marzipan)
1kg (2lb) deep turquoise sugarpaste (rolled fondant)
125g (4oz) Mexican Paste (2), see page 6
500g (1lb) white mexican paste
250g (8oz/1 cup) white royal icing
Deep turquoise paste food colour
Sugar glue

Equipment

28cm (11 inch) round cake board
Tracing paper and pencil
Thin card for template
Scriber
Craft knife or scalpel
Dresden tool
Nos. 1 and 1.5 piping tubes (tips)
Piping bags
Paintbrush

Cutters

Small and medium lace leaf cutters (OP, LL3 (47mm), LL4 (40mm))

Preparation

1 Coat the cake board with deep turquoise sugarpaste and allow to set. Brush the cake with apricot glaze and coat with almond paste. Cover with deep turquoise sugarpaste and allow to dry for 24 hours. Place the cake in the centre of the covered board. Using turquoise royal icing and a no. 1.5 piping tube, pipe a snail's trail to neaten the join between the cake and the board.

Peacock bodies

2 Trace the peacock bodies (see page 47), then transfer to thin card and cut out to make templates.

3 Make a paper template of the top of the cake, showing the position of the peacocks. Place on the cake and mark the outlines of the peacocks on the cake with a scriber. At the same time, mark faint guidelines for the tails.

4 Roll out the Mexican Paste (2) approximately 5mm (¼ inch) thick. Cut out the peacock bodies using the card templates and a craft knife or scalpel. Smooth the edges of the

bodies with your fingertips to give them a rounded appearance. Using a dresden tool, mark details on the heads and beaks.

5 While the bodies are still slightly soft, stick them into position on the top of the cake with a little sugar glue.

Peacock tails

6 Roll out the white mexican paste thinly and cut out lace leaf pieces in different

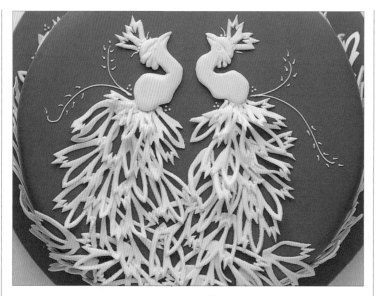

scribed guidelines, always working in the same direction and overlapping the leaves as you work. As the pieces are soft you will be able to bend and turn them to create movement. Use the paintbrush to help you do this.Gradually increase the width of the tails as you get nearer to the bodies. Where the tails overlap, intertwine the pieces, alternating from side to side.

Finishing

8 > Fix a few extra small lace pieces to the base of the peacock bodies to finish off, and attach small lace pieces to the tops of the heads to represent crowns.

9 > With a no. 1 piping tube and white royal icing, finish the design with a few piped lines and dots.

sizes. Some pieces can be reduced by trimming them with a sharp knife. You will need 50–100 pieces in total. After you have cut them out, keep the lace pieces covered to prevent them from drying out.

7 > Starting at the back of the cake, and using a little royal icing, fix several lace leaves to the board, pointing away from each other. Gradually work around the board and up the side of the cake following the

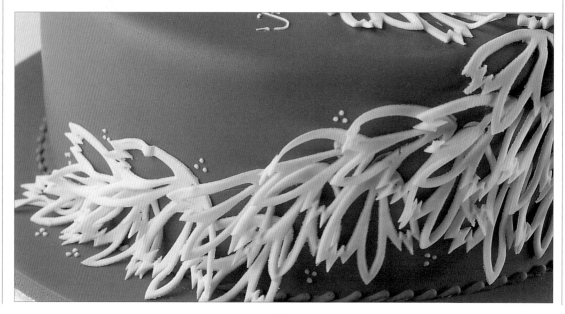

Town Houses

Create your own town or village with geometric cutters. Let your imagination run away with you, you could even include a duck pond (complete with ducks)!

Materials

25cm (10 inch) long octagonal cake
Apricot glaze
750g (1½lb) almond paste (marzipan)
1kg (2lb) sugarpaste (rolled fondant)
750g (1½lb) mexican paste
500g (1lb/2 cups) royal icing
Selection of paste and powder food colours
Clear alcohol (vodka or white rum)

Equipment

30cm (12 inch) long octagonal cake board
Dresden tool
Paintbrush
Strip of paper
Craft knife or scalpel
Nos. 1, 1.5 and 2 piping tubes (tips)
Piping bags
Soft brush for dusting

Cutters

Selection of small square cutters (FCC, 625 – set of 4)
Selection of small rectangular cutters (FCC, 465 – set of 4)
Several small leaf and flower cutters

Preparation

1 Coat the cake board with white sugarpaste, and, while the paste is still soft, mark areas around the edge with a dresden tool or the edge of a ruler to give a 'paved' or 'tiled' effect. Allow to set.

2 Brush the cake with apricot glaze and cover with almond paste. Coat with white sugarpaste and allow to set. Place the cake centrally on the board.

Houses

3 Colour the mexican paste in a selection of different colours for the houses. I have chosen to make the houses in

various colours but black and white would be equally effective.

4 Measure the circumference of the cake, and cut out a strip of paper that will go around it. Arrange the cutters along the strip and work out how many houses you need to make.

a sharp knife. Cut out all the pieces you will need, mark them with doors, windows, roof tiles, etc., using a dresden tool, or embossing them with small cutters, and allow to dry. Paint the pieces as required, using powder colours mixed with clear alcohol. Keep each house and its component parts separate to prevent getting muddled.

5 Roll out the paste thinly and cut out pieces with which to make the houses. Make them all as different as possible. Triangular roofs can be made by cutting squares diagonally with

6 Assemble the pieces using royal icing and a no. 1 piping tube, and allow to dry. Some details can be added in royal icing at this stage – door knobs, flowers, climbing roses and vines, etc. These can be finished off when the houses have been fixed to the cake.

Assembly

7 Using piped royal icing, fix the houses to the cake, some flat against the sides, others standing out from the cake. Put in side walls and gable ends if you wish.

8 Roll out some mexican paste and make some small trees and shrubs using leaf and flower cutters. Allow to dry, then fix in position with royal icing. Add final details with royal icing, or by painting, and dust with colour, on the houses and the paving.

Fantasy Collar Cake

Pretty cut-outs are used to form a collar on this cake. The same cutter has been used to make the top and side decorations.

Materials

25cm (10 inch) oval cake
Apricot glaze
750g (1½lb) almond paste (marzipan)
1kg (2lb) pale pink sugarpaste (rolled fondant)
500g (1lb) mexican paste
Pink and cream paste food colours
500g (1lb) royal icing
Selection of powder food colours
Clear alcohol
Sugar glue

Equipment

30cm (12 inch) oval cake board
Craft knife or scalpel
Nos. 0 and 1 piping tubes (tips)
Piping bags
Pieces of foam

Cutters

Embroidery cutter (Guy, Paul & Co: JEM, EC-3)
10cm (4 inch) oval plaque cutter

Preparation

1 Coat the cake board with pink sugarpaste and allow to dry. Brush the cake with apricot glaze and coat with almond paste. Cover with pink sugarpaste and allow to dry.

Embroidery cut-outs

2 Colour the mexican paste the same pale pink as the sugarpaste. Roll out the paste thinly and cut out eight shapes (six for the collar; two for the top decoration) with the embroidery cutter. Trim the centre 'curl' from the base of two of the cut-outs with a sharp knife to give them a level base. Leave all the pieces on a foam pad to dry.

3 Cut an oval plaque out of the pink paste with the plaque cutter. Allow to dry.

4 Cut out several more embroidery pieces. Following the illustrations on page 48, cut the pieces into sections with a sharp knife. Curve and shape the individual pieces and allow to dry.

Side decoration

5 Cut out another six embroidery shapes and trim the bases with a sharp knife (as in Step 2) to ensure they will fit neatly around the base of the cake. Cover the pieces to prevent them from drying out too quickly.

6 While the pieces are still soft, fix them around the sides of the cake with sugar glue, making sure they just touch the board. Cut out some

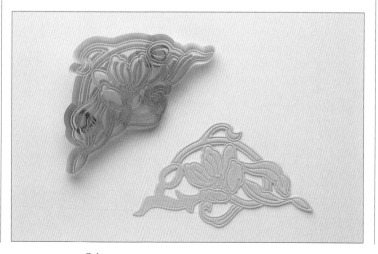

more embroidery pieces and cut them into sections (as in Step 4). Stick some of the small sections on the side of the cake and the board, between the large embroidery pieces.

7 Using cream-coloured royal icing and nos. 0 and 1 piping tubes, pipe embroidery between the cut-outs on the side of the cake and on the board. The cut-outs can also be over-piped or painted with food colours or brush-embroidered.

Collar

8 Paint and/or pipe the six cut-outs for the collar, if necessary, to match the side decoration. Allow to dry.

9 Fix the cut-outs to the top edge of the cake with a little pink royal icing, allowing about 4cm (1½ inches) of each cut-out to project over the edge of the cake. Gently move the cut-outs, overlapping them if necessary, until they fit neatly all the way around.

Top decoration

10 Stick the two remaining cut-outs together, back-to-back (reversing one of them), with a little royal icing. Allow to dry.

11 Stand the piece in the centre of the oval plaque and fix with royal icing. Support with pieces of foam until dry.

12 Pipe and/or paint in any extra details you wish, so that all the cut-outs on the cake match. Repeat for the individual sections previously cut out and shaped in Step 4.

13 Add the extra sections to both sides of the centre ornament, arranging them to look like flowers and leaves. Support with foam until dry. Pipe dots in the centres of the flowers. Carefully lift the top decoration on to the centre of the cake and fix with royal icing.

Russian Wedding Cake

The spectacular domes of St Basil's Cathedral in Moscow are echoed in the curved and elegant lines of this wedding cake. Other cutters such as large lilies or rose petals could be used to make the side decorations.

Materials

18cm (7 inch) and 25cm (10 inch) round cakes
Apricot glaze
2kg (4lb) almond paste (marzipan)
2kg (4lb) ivory sugarpaste (rolled fondant)
750g (1½lb) mexican paste .
500g (1lb/2 cups) royal icing
Ivory paste food colour
Sugar glue

Equipment

25cm (10 inch) and 33cm (13 inch) round cake boards
Ruler
Craft knife or scalpel
10cm (4 inch) diameter cardboard tube
Nos. 1, 1.5 and 2 piping tubes (tips)
Piping bags
Pieces of foam
Curved former
4 Perspex pillars or dowels

Cutters

Arum/calla lily cutters in 4 sizes (JEM B42, 56, 55, 54)
10cm (4 inch) round plaque cutter

Preparation

1 Coat the cake boards with ivory sugarpaste. Brush the cakes with apricot glaze and cover with almond paste. Allow to set for 24 hours.

2 Coat the cakes with ivory sugarpaste. Place the cakes on the sugarpasted boards and allow to set for 24 hours.

The spacer

3 Colour the mexican paste with ivory food colour the same shade as the sugarpaste on the cake and boards. Roll out to approximately 2.5mm (⅛ inch) thick and cut out a strip 30cm (12 inches) long and 4.5cm (1¾ inches) wide. Using the smallest lily cutter (54), carefully cut out and remove petal shapes from the strip, spacing them evenly around the strip and reversing the direction of the cutter each time.

4 Carefully wrap the strip around the cardboard tube, making sure that the ends meet neatly. Leave to dry.

5 Join the two ends of the spacer together with ivory royal icing. Keep the spacer supported by the tube until you are ready to assemble the cakes.

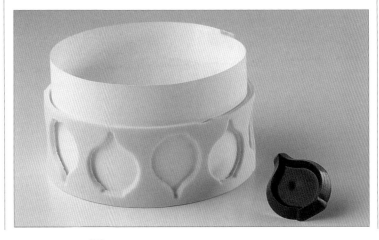

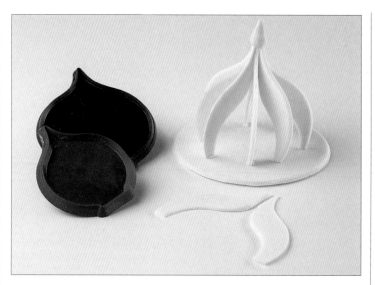

Top decoration

6 ▷ Roll out some mexican paste and cut out a 10cm (4 inch) plaque. Leave to dry.

7 ▷ Roll out some more paste and cut out four petal shapes with the largest lily cutter (B42). Remove the centres of the shapes with the next smallest cutter (56), and, with a sharp knife, cut all the pieces straight across the bases. Cut three of the pieces in half, leaving one whole, and allow to dry.

8 ▷ Using a very little ivory royal icing, fix the pieces together at the top points and on to the plaque. Add a small cone of ivory paste to the top of the arrangement. Support with pieces of foam while drying.

Side decorations

9 ▷ Roll out some more mexican paste and cut out shapes with the smallest cutter (54). Place these over a curved former with the bases flat and the tips curling over, so that they will fit neatly against the sides of the cake. Allow to dry.

10 ▷ Roll out more mexican paste and cut out petal shapes with the second largest cutter (56). Remove the centres from these with the next size down (55). Keep all these pieces covered to prevent them from drying out too quickly.

11 ▷ While the petal pieces are still pliable, attach the

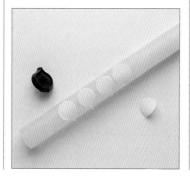

largest to the sides of the cakes with a little sugar glue, spacing them evenly. Bend and shape them gently so that they follow the curve of the cakes.

12 ▷ Fix the flat petal shapes on to the cakes with royal icing, positioning them over and in between the pieces already in place and gently curling the tips over. Allow to dry. Fix the small curved shapes to the sides of the large cake with royal icing, again positioning them over the shapes already in place. Allow to dry.

13 ▷ Add teardrops and extra piping with ivory royal icing and a no. 2 piping tube.

Assembly

14 ▷ Measure the height of the large cake, plus the height of the spacer, plus 2.5mm (⅛ inch). Cut the Perspex pillars or dowels to the measured length and smooth any rough edges.

15 ▷ Carefully insert the dowels into the large cake and slip the spacer over the top. The dowels should project approximately 2.5mm (⅛ inch) above the spacer. This is to protect the spacer when the top cake is placed in position.

16 ▷ Fix the top decoration to the small cake with royal icing and, with a no. 2 piping tube, neaten the edge with a snail's trail. Leave to dry, then carefully place the small cake on top of the large one, resting it on the dowels above the spacer.

Teddy Bear Cake

Everyone loves teddy bears and this cake will be doubly popular with marzipan and chocolate lovers! Other animal cutters could be used in the same way.

Materials

20cm (8 inch) hexagonal chocolate cake
Apricot glaze
625g (1¼lb) almond paste
(marzipan)
500g (1lb) chocolate-flavoured
sugarpaste (rolled fondant)
500g (1lb) Marzipan Modelling
Paste, see page 6
250g (8oz/1 cup) chocolate-
coloured royal icing
Brown powder food colour (petal
dust/blossom tint)
30g (1oz) mexican paste
Blue paste food colouring
Sugar glue

Equipment

28cm (11 inch) hexagonal cake
board
Nos. 1.5 and 2 piping tubes (tips)
Piping bags
Stiff card and pencil
Soft brush for dusting

Cutters

Large, medium and small bear
cutters (PME, TB498, TB499, TB
500)
90mm (3½ inch) oval plaque
cutter
Plain round briar rose cutters
(PME)
Ribbon cutter (FCC)

Preparation

1 Blend 500g (1lb) almond paste with 250g (8oz) chocolate sugarpaste to create a marbled effect. Brush the cake with apricot glaze and cover with marbled paste. Allow to set for 24 hours.

Board and plaque

2 Coat the cake board with chocolate sugarpaste and cut out and remove bear shapes around the edge with the small bear cutter. Roll out the remaining 125g (4oz) almond paste and cut out bear shapes with the same cutter. Fix the almond paste bears into the cut-out spaces on the board and smooth over gently to seal.

3 Re-roll the almond paste trimmings and cut out an oval plaque using the plaque cutter. Leave to dry.

4 Place the cake in the centre of the covered board. Using chocolate-coloured royal icing and a no. 2 piping tube, pipe a small snail's trail to seal the edge of the cake to the board.

5 Fix the almond paste plaque to the top of the cake with a little royal icing.

Using chocolate-coloured royal icing and a no. 1.5 piping tube, pipe a snail's trail around the edge of the plaque.

Bears

6 Roll out the marzipan modelling paste to approximately 2.5mm (⅛ inch) thick, and cut out 20 bears using the medium bear cutter. Allow to dry in a warm place for at least 48 hours. You may not need all 20 bears, but it is useful to have some 'spares' in case of breakages.

7 Roll out some more paste and cut out two bears using the large bear cutter, and three discs (one of each size) using the briar rose cutters. Also cut out a small triangular piece of paste as a support for the top decoration. Remove the arms and legs from one of the large bears using a craft knife or scalpel. Allow all the pieces to dry flat in a warm place for at least 48 hours.

8 Assemble the large bear by placing the different pieces one on top of the other, separated by small dots of royal icing. Allow the icing to dry before adding the next layer. Leave to dry for 24 hours.

9 Dust the bear with brown powder food colour. With chocolate-coloured royal icing and a no. 1.5 piping tube, pipe in facial details and paw pads. Colour the mexican paste blue, roll it out very thinly and cut into strips with the ribbon cutter. Shape a bow (see page 16) and attach to the bear.

Assembly

10 Using a pencil and stiff card, draw around the medium bear cutter and cut out the shape. Use this template to indent the position of the feet for the marzipan bears on the sugarpasted board. This will help to support the bears.

11 Using chocolate-coloured royal icing and a no. 2 piping tube, pipe a little royal icing into the indentations on the board and set the paste bears into them. Support with small pieces of foam or sugar lumps until set.

12 Finally, fix the large bear to the top of the cake using the same method as in steps 10 and 11. Add the triangular piece of paste to support the bear from the back.

Black Lacquerwork Cake

The design of this dramatic cake is very reminiscent of oriental lacquerwork. A number of different cutters are used to make the appliqué pieces, which are then smoothed and contoured to give the impression of relief.

Materials

20cm (8 inch) scalloped oval cake
Apricot glaze
750g (1½lb) almond paste (marzipan)
1kg (2lb) black sugarpaste (rolled fondant)
250g (8oz) Mexican Paste (1), see page 5
500g (1lb) Mexican Paste (2), see page 6
250g (8oz/1 cup) black royal icing
Black paste food colouring
Red, green and gold powder food colours (petal dusts/blossom tints)
Copper and soft gold edible lustre dust
Sugar glue

Equipment

25cm (10 inch) scalloped oval cake board
Tracing paper and pencil
Thin card for template
Craft knife or scalpel
10cm (4 inch) diameter cardboard tube
Paintbrushes
Dresden tool
Nos. 0, 1 and 1.5 piping tubes (tips)
Piping bags

Cutters

Approx 13x4cm (5½x1½ inch) border cutter (OP, LB1)
Small rectangular cutter
Selection of leaf cutters, including geranium and chrysanthemum
Ribbon cutter (FCC, 245)

Preparation

1 Coat the board with black sugarpaste and allow to set. Brush the cake with apricot glaze and cover with almond paste. Coat with black sugarpaste and allow to dry for 24 hours. Set the cake in the centre of the board.

Note

When working with very dark colours use the minimum amount of icing (confectioner's) sugar for rolling out to prevent any discolouration of the paste. Small pieces of dark paste can be rolled out on a little white vegetable fat (shortening).

Border off-pieces

2 Trace the template for the cut-out centre of the border off-pieces on page 47, and transfer to thin card. Cut out to make a template. (You could use a small cutter to remove this cut-out if you prefer.)

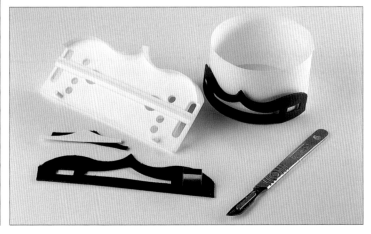

up the flower pattern all around the cake in the same way.

7 Thinly roll out some black Mexican Paste (1) and use the ribbon cutter to cut out reeds. Trim the ends of the pieces to points with a sharp knife, and mark a vein down the centre of each one with the dresden tool.

8 Dust the pieces with greens and golds, as before, and allow some to dry in natural curves. Fix the straight reeds directly on to the cake and board while still soft. When the curved reeds are dry, fix them to the cake with a little black royal icing.

9 Cut more ribbon strips to make stems. Colour as required and attach to the side of the cake between the leaf and flower arrangements.

10 With nos. 0 and 1 piping tubes and black royal icing, add any small details to finish the design, e.g. stamens, etc. Fix the border sections to the top of the cake with a little black royal icing.

3 Thinly roll out some black Mexican Paste (1) and cut out four pieces using the border cutter. Cut out the centre sections using the template and a sharp knife. Cut out a small rectangle on either side of the centre cut-out section. Set these pieces to dry around a 10cm (4 inch) cardboard tube.

Leaves

4 Roll out some black Mexican Paste (2) and cut out several leaves using the geranium and chrysanthemum leaf cutters. Separate the sections of the geranium leaves with a sharp knife. Keep all the pieces covered as much as possible to prevent them drying out.

5 Dust all the leaf pieces with your chosen colours and 'fix' the colours by rubbing gently with the ball of your finger. Add a little copper or soft gold lustre to the sections after they have been coloured.

6 Working with the paste while it is still soft, and starting with leaf shapes in green, fix the pieces to the cake with a little sugar glue, overlapping them where necessary. Smooth into position with your fingertips, making sure that the edges are rounded and that they blend into the surface of the cake. Where necessary, use a dresden tool to indent around the edges of the design and to create veins. Continue to build

44

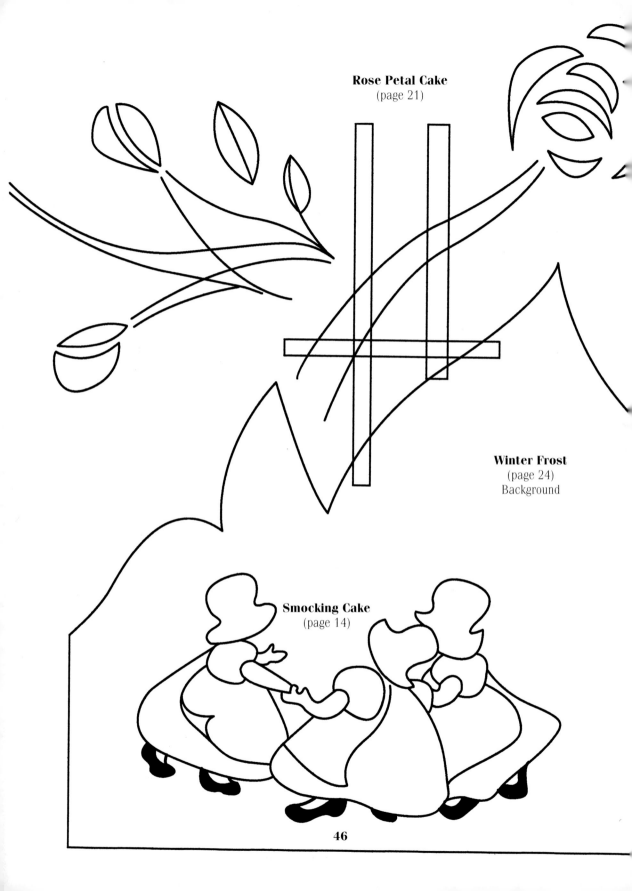

Rose Petal Cake
(page 21)

Winter Frost
(page 24)
Background

Smocking Cake
(page 14)

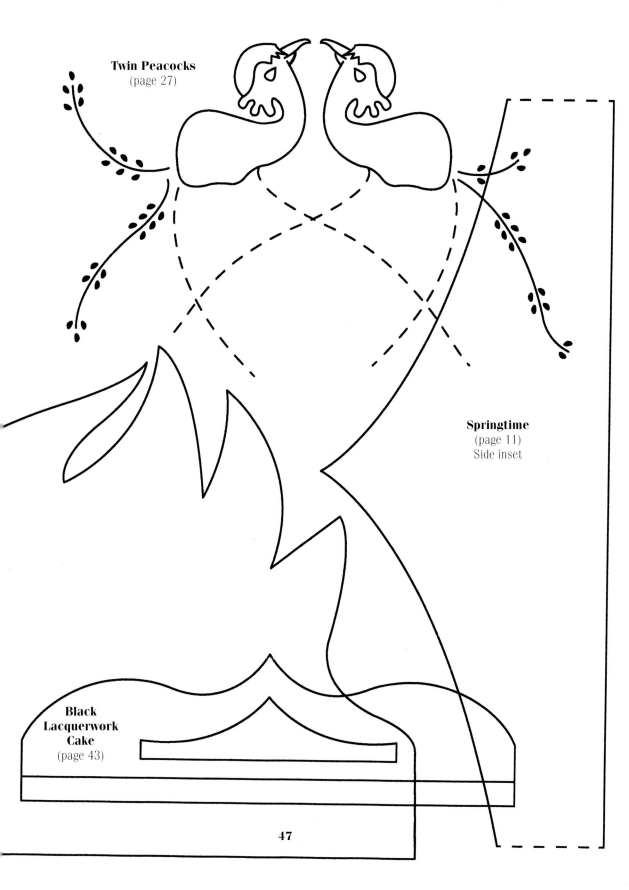

Twin Peacocks
(page 27)

Springtime
(page 11)
Side inset

**Black
Lacquerwork
Cake**
(page 43)

Fantasy Collar Cake
(page 34)

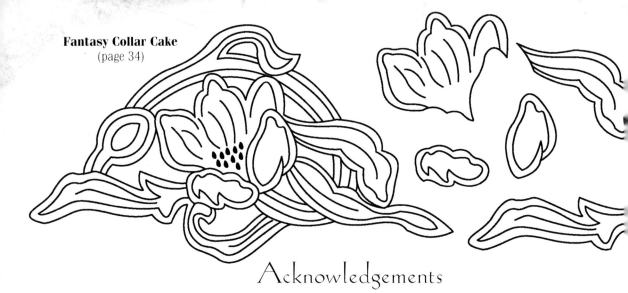

Acknowledgements

I would like to thank everyone who has made this book possible: my family and friends for their continued support, and, in particular, my husband Dave for his help, advice and encouragement; Lynn for the tea and the typing and the laughter; and Barbara for making a long-held dream into a reality.

The author and publishers would also like to thank the following manufacturers and suppliers:

Patchwork Cutters (PC)
3 Raines Close, Greasby
Wirral L49 2QB

Fine Cut Cutters (FCC)
Workshop 2
Old Stables Block
Holme Pierrepoint Hall
Holme Pierrepoint
Nottingham NG12 2LD

Orchard Products (OP)
51 Hallyburton Road
Hove
East Sussex BN3 7GP

P.M.E. Sugarcraft (PME)
Brember Road
South Harrow
Middlesex HA2 8UN

Guy Paul & Co Ltd (GP)
Unit B4, Foundry Way
Little End Road
Eaton Socon
Cambs PE19 3JH

Cornish Cake Boards (CCB)
Garth-an-deys, Rosehill
Goonhaven, Truro
Cornwall TR4 9JT

Artgato (AG)
5 Avenue du Dr Arnold Netter
75012 Paris, France

Country Cutters (CC)
Lower Trefoldu, Dingeston
Monmouth, Gwent NP5 4BQ

Cake Art Ltd (CA)
Venture Way, Crown Estate
Priorswood, Taunton
Somerset TA2 8DE

J.F. Renshaw Ltd (JFR)
Crown Street
Liverpool L8 7RF

Anniversary House (Cake Decorations) Ltd (AH)
Unit 5
Roundways
Elliott Road
Bournemouth
Hants BH11 8JJ

Squires Kitchen (SK)
Squires House
3 Waverley Lane, Farnham
Surrey GU9 8BB

Australian cake decoration suppliers:

Cake Decorators' Supplies
Shop 1, 770 George Street
Sydney 2001   Tel: 92124050

Westernhagen AE & Co.
22–24 Addison Road
Marrickville 2204   Tel: 9557039

Hollywood Cake Decorations
52 Beach Street
Kogarah   Tel: 9587 1533

Candyman Cake Decorating Equipment
7 Parkes Street
Manly Vale   Tel: 9949 6735

The Cake Connection
Shop 5, Castle Plaza
273 Old Northern Road
Castle Hill   Tel: 9899 3065

Bakery Sugar Craft
Unit 4, 1 Cowpasture Place
Wetherill Park   Tel: 9756 6164